The Smart Business Owners Guide to

Basic Accounting

(Or, Keep it Simple Silly)

Learn How to Do Your Books in Less Than an

Hour Per Week

Nina Register, CPA

Table of Contents

Introduction

As a brand-new Business Owner, you have learned about affiliate programs and/or creating your own products, auto responders, hosting services, building a webpage or mini-site and a host of other items, but now comes the truly scary part: Accounting for Everything!

Well, I am here to take you by the hand and make your life easier. You will not only learn what you need to do and how to do it, but you will also know what the various accounting terms mean and be able to hold your own in any business conversation. Assuming your eyes don't glaze over first.

A new world of possibilities is about to open, and it will set you free. So, let the journey begin ...

What is Accounting

I am sure you have heard the terms accounting and bookkeeping, and you have probably thought that they are basically the same. Well, in some ways they are, because you can't have accounting without bookkeeping, but you can have bookkeeping without accounting.

Bookkeeping is exactly what it says it is, keeping the books. It is the equivalent of a check register. For those of you under a certain age, this is what we used to write down every check we wrote or every deposit we made. I know most people don't do this anymore, but there is an online equivalent. It shows all the ins and outs of your account, but it does not tell your how your business is really doing.

Accounting on the other hand takes all that information as well as sales and marketing information, human resources information, insurance information and many other items and give you the "big picture" of your business by creating financial statements. These statements can then be used for all types of things. They can be used to talk to your banker for the future growth of your company. The financials can be used to help minimize your tax liability. They can also be used to help determine your personal and business needs as your business grows.

The bottom line on all of this is if you do not pay attention to your books, your will not know if you are even making any money never mind how much money you may be making. Even worse, you may not even realize some of the things you are doing are actually costing you money. But do not worry, there is help out there to make this easier for the smart Business Owner.

Let Your Checkbook Be Your Guide

For the majority of Business Owners, you will probably be selling some sort of digital information product: an e-Book, Video/Video Course or Audio/Audio course and will not have any physical inventory. If you do have a physical product, I would suggest using some sort of fulfillment service, so you do not have to carry a physical inventory if that is possible. It makes life a lot easier. If you are selling on Etsy, Shopify or Amazon, you will need to have inventory. It may be a POD (print on demand) or a drop ship type of inventory which means you do not have boxes of stuff in your garage. Assuming this is the case, you operate what is considered by accountants and the IRS as a cash basis business or possibly a modified accrual basis. This means that you record revenues (money coming in) when it is received and record expenses (money going out) when you spend it. This is in essence what you do with your checkbook. You record your paychecks (or other receipts such as interest or dividends) when they come in and you record your checks as you write them. Or these days, when you use your debit/credit card. Then you know how much money you have. To be a true cash basis business, you would not be able to pay for supplies or other items with your credit cards or lines of credit unless it is paid within thirty days. Nor would you be able to get your money through ClickBank, JV Zoo, Warrior Plus or PayPal. Selling items through eBay is more in line with a true cash basis business or if you use something like Stripe or Square and get your fund in just a few days.

.

Now, for example if you were to sell an eBook through ClickBank or Amazon the money shows up in your account there immediately after the customer provides their credit/debit card information. Granted it might take a couple of weeks to actually get the funds from them, but it is in your account and as far as the IRS is concerned and this is a completed sale (this is where the modified part comes in).

If you go to the store and buy office supplies (even if you charge the purchase on your credit card, that modified part again) that expense is incurred on that date and needs to be recorded on that date, not the date that your pay the credit card company. Note: if you do pay by credit card, a good way to control expenses is to write the amount in your checkbook or some sort of log on that date as if you wrote a check and then you will have the funds available when the credit card bill needs to be paid. Also, it will help you from spending more than you have in the bank.

Now, by recording all your revenue or sales and expenses in your checkbook, you have a log that is easy to follow, and you know if you have any money left at the end of the day. Or, you can take your bank and credit card statement and see if you have spent more than your earned.

One other note, it is best to have a separate bank account and debit/credit card that is used exclusively in the business. This way you are not comingling your personal and business funds.

Hopefully, you will have some left, but in the startup phase those numbers may be in the red.

Why You Don't Need Expensive Software

If you have been in any office supply store (or bookstore) lately you will see several types of accounting and/or tax software and they will be priced from a few dollars to several hundred dollars.

I am here to tell you that they are not necessary. Also, most are not designed with the online Business Owner in mind. They are still focused on the traditional brick and mortar types of businesses. Your best bet is a spreadsheet software. Most computers these days come preloaded with all types of software and it usually includes some type of spreadsheet software. This is all you really need. (Note: the author assumes you know how to use a basic spreadsheet software such as Microsoft Excel™ or Google™ Sheets. Teaching you how to use the software basics is beyond the scope of this book).

Now most small Business Owners are going to be what is considered a sole proprietorship (otherwise known as a one man or *one woman* show). You might think that if you have any employees you must use these pre-packaged softwares. *Au contraire,* you can do payroll with a basic spreadsheet software and most banks these day will let you set up a wire transfer to a specific account i.e. the IRS or an employee so that you can even offer direct deposit to an employee. Now if you are getting up into the 10+ employee range, I would suggest outsourcing your payroll to a service that specializes in payroll. It just makes sense and will save you tons of time. Also, is you are using a non-US based VA (virtual assistant), they are not considered employees, but are considered contract workers and as such, their fees are just a normal operating expense not payroll.

You can also do sales tax calculation on a simple spreadsheet, whether you include the sales tax in the price of the item or calculate it as a separate item. If you are using any online 3rd party firms to sell and/or deliver your product like Amazon, they will take taxes out for you.

Another advantage of spreadsheets is that you are not obligated to buy updates from the software companies every year, especially the tax modules. Our friendly government entities are more than happy to let you download any tax form or their related instructions at IRS.gov. So, the spreadsheet software should become your best friend.

Putting it All Together

Now, you have made all these spreadsheets from your checkbook, your payroll and payroll taxes (if needed) and your sales taxes (if needed), but here comes the big question: NOW WHAT?

Never fear, with the information you now have in your hot little hands, you can put together what accountants call: Financial Statements. The three basic financial statements are: The Balance Sheet, the Income Statement and the General Ledger. Another good report to have is a Statement of Cash Flows, but that is not necessary unless your company becomes a full-fledged accrual basis business, which won't happen unless you are an inventory only type of business.

The first statement to work on is the General Ledger. It is the statement that lists all those checkbook or debit/credit card transactions. It will also include payroll, payroll taxes (both employer and employee portions) and any sales taxes, if necessary.

This will then show everything you received, everything you paid and everything you may still owe (read payroll and/or sales taxes and credit card balances). You will need to add every item in each revenue or expense category to come up with a total. These numbers will then be transferred to the Income Statement. As you input these numbers on your general ledger, every line must equal zero. See Exhibit A.

The sum of the revenues and expenses will then give you your net income/<loss>. This statement reflects activity for a specific period of time, usually a month, quarter or the entire year. See Exhibit B.

The balance of your cash account from the General Ledger and any capital items (computers, equipment, cars or land and buildings) you may have purchased will go on your Balance Sheet as an Asset. If you owe anyone such as credit card balance or taxes this will go on the liability section of your balance Sheet. NOTE: your cash account and your credit card account **MUST** match (balance) to the statements you receive from your bank or credit card company. There may be fees or interest that you would otherwise miss if you do not match exactly. Your Net Income/<Loss> will also go on the Balance Sheet, but it goes in the Liabilities and Equity section. If you have a loss, you will need to show some sort of liability or capital contributions so that the asset side (cash and other items) equals the liability and equity section. Usually, if you are a sole proprietor you have paid for things out of your own pocket and this would be your capital contribution. This statement reflects your financial position as of a specific date and only for that specific date. See Exhibit C

But, What Does It All Mean?

A set of financial statements can tell someone quite a lot about a business. First it can tell if the business is making money. Second, it can tell how a business is making money. Third, it can tell how a business is spending its money.

First, is the business making any money? Obviously, most people start a business to make money. Your intent may only be to have a second income, but you still want to make more than you spend. Also, we all have our philanthropic sides, but not at the expense of our livelihoods. Now it is expected that a start-up business will lose money, especially in the beginning, because it takes time and money to build a client list and get enough sales. That is why the IRS allows you to have a loss for 3 of the first 5 years before they come knocking on your door and tell you that "NO, you do not have a business, you have a hobby" and they want you to recapture all those losses and then pay taxes and interest on them. Ouch!

Second, how is the business making money? Does the business sell more than one type of item? Is item #2 selling better than item #1? Or vice a versa? Does the business any items as a loss leader? All these questions and more can be determined from your income statement.

Third, how is the business spending its money? Does it cost more to produce the item than what it is being sold for? Does it cost more to advertise the item for sale than the item is being sold for (think Google advertising or FB ads)? Is the owner/manager taking out or spending more money on him or herself that the business can support?

There are a lot of nuggets of information that can be mined from these three basic financial statements of a business. Also, there are a variety of ratios that can used to analyze the data and to find out even more information about the health of a business.

Taxes, Taxes and More Taxes

(or, Why We all Fear the IRS)

There are three main types of taxes that every business in the USA, large or small, must deal with: Federal Income Tax, Payroll Tax (if you have any employees) and State Sales Tax (if you sell a physical product or even some types of services). You may also be subject to a state income tax or state franchise tax depending on where you live and what type of business you have.

Now, it is no mystery why everyone fears the IRS. The IRS itself fosters this belief and our Congress is right behind them. It they didn't, people would not be interested in paying their taxes and then all the bureaucrats would not get paid (hmmm . . . maybe there's something to that). Well, our society is structured in this fashion and it behooves us to learn the laws and to maximize the benefits we can receive.

The first thing to remember is yes, you do have to pay taxes, however, the way the tax laws are written, there are always gray areas and you can do your best to achieve tax minimization.

Now as a business owner, you have many things that you can use to help minimize your taxes. These include the home office deduction as well as all the basic business operating expenses that any brick-and-mortar business would it be able to take.

Of course, there is one thing to fear from the IRS and that is an audit. However, if you follow this book and keep good records an IRS auditor will hopefully never have any reason to visit you.

Most everyone knows to keep receipts and how to make the most of the few deductions that the IRS allows, for example: mortgage interest, charitable deductions and schooling expenses. For the new business owner, especially the home-based Business

Owner, a whole new world of possibilities has just opened up to you.

The main tax break that is available for a new home-based business is drum roll please: The Home Office Deduction. You've got to love the creativity at the IRS for some of the names on these forms.

This deduction means exactly what it sounds like. It allows you to write-off the cost of operating and maintaining that part of your home that is used *"exclusively"* for business. This could include a portion of your rent or mortgage, utilities, trash collection and security system. But note, the IRS is pretty picky about that exclusive condition. You can't take a spare bedroom and put a desk and chair in there and expect to take the whole room for the deduction. As far as the IRS is concerned, that spare bed makes it a bedroom, NOT an office, so be careful how you calculate the deduction. Now if you are lucky enough to have a detached garage or separate building on your property (say a shed) that you convert into an office, you would have an easier time taking all the cost allocated to the building. The other thing to remember with the home office deduction is that you cannot take it if you already have a net loss before the deduction.

In addition to the home-office deduction, there are all sorts of cost that can be written off in the normal course of doing business. These could include computers, office supplies, a second phone line, hosting services autoresponders, travel expenses and much, much more. One note here, you must have a second phone line to take the phone expense even if you have cell phones. Note, this is only for the home-office deduction. The IRS is pretty specific about it not being a home phone. If you have a physical office elsewhere, there is no issue with taking the phone expense for that location.

As always you should consult your Accountant or Tax Advisor to learn how these advantages could apply to you and your business especially since some things could vary from state to state.

5 Tips to Prevent an Audit

As much as any accountant or tax advisor hates to admit it, there is always the possibility of an IRS audit. Now the likelihood is very, very small, but they do happen.

The following is a list of items that might get you audited. But remember, "may the odds be ever in your favor".

❖ The home office deduction. This is considered a red flag. There have been a lot of abuses in this area. Now most advisers will tell you that this is a great deduction and it is, but you must be conservative and document everything and keep those documents for a minimum of 3 years after the tax year.

❖ Sole proprietors whose main income is tips or mostly cash. This is another area where there have been many abuses, especially since there's a lot of cash involved. The IRS calculates an average earnings per day based on some formula that they have determined, and they look for reported income to be in that range.

❖ Businesses that could be considered recreational or hobbies. These are businesses like raising horses or craft shows or internet marketing. A lot of people do these things anyway and you would have to show that you really do this for a living and not just as a weekend or entertainment type thing.

❖ Large deductions relative to your income. For example, if your charitable donations, travel or meals and entertainment are more than 50% of what you earn the IRS is going to wonder how you can afford to live.

❖ A self-employed person who has incorporated themselves and whose annual net income exceeds $250,000. Enough said

You can reduce your risk of an audit by:

➢ Answer all questions on the tax return, otherwise known as filling in the blanks.

➢ Using exact numbers not round numbers. For example: $4,573 instead of $5,000

➢ Double check all your math to find any errors (so the IRS doesn't!)

➢ Preparing a neat and legible return. There's nothing worse than a sloppy return that is handwritten and that you didn't fill everything you need to fill in or that you can't read. it is so easy these days to go to IRS.gov, open the form that you need and just fill in the blanks on their site. All you have to do after that is just print out a pretty copy that is all done and sign.

➢ Attaching explanations for any item that might be considered questionable. It's definitely easier to explain something before rather than after. If the IRS can't understand why you did something, they will send you a notice, there will be a bill with interest and penalties that will continue to increase until they agree to your explanation or not. Trying to backtrack and get something fixed is always harder than doing it correctly the first go-round. This is not the time for asking forgiveness instead of permission.

Now obviously there are no guarantees about what the IRS is looking for in any particular year. but taking care of things as outlined above and keeping good records will probably help and always keep your records for at least 3 years after the tax year and sometimes as much as 7 years.

Should You Hire an Accountant or Tax Advisor?

Well you usually don't need one the day you start your business. Actually, you may never need one depending on the size and scope of your business, but just like any professional (doctor, lawyer, car mechanic or computer repair person) you should not wait until you need one before you go looking for one. It never fails that you can just end up spending too much money and most of the time it is not a good fit.

I strongly suggest that you do your own books (or a family member you can trust absolutely) especially in the beginning. Now this may only be for the first few months, but this will help you understand your business. Accounting is just one more tool in your arsenal to help you build a successful business.

Eventually as your business grows you may want to hire an accountant or a tax advisor to help you keep growing your business and protect the assets of that business. This could range from making sure you maximize all those tax deductions, investment planning, estate planning and eventually to possibly have a succession plan. You do want to retire someday enjoy the fruits of your labor, don't you?

When you are ready for that help here are a few things you should look for:

- ❖ Are they a CPA? Or do they have some other certification?
- ❖ Are they experienced in your industry and the size of your business?
- ❖ Do they have references from a banker or another business owner?
- ❖ Are they easily accessible? Do they return your calls or emails in a timely manner? You do not want to have to hunt them down every time you need something answered. Remember though that you are not their only client and it may take some time, but not weeks.

❖ Can they help you with other issues of your business? This could be finding you the right insurance/Insurance Agent. If you grow big enough and you eventually do want that brick-and-mortar can they help you find a real estate agent that you can work with? Obviously commercial real estate is different than residential and let's face it most times when you're looking for a real estate agent, you're going to find residential not commercial and lastly,

❖ Are you comfortable with them?

Remember when all is said and done the Accountant or Tax Advisor works for you not the other way around. They should respect

your business knowledge and the experience
you have in your industry.

Some Basic Accounting Terms

If you have ever tried to figure out what the accountant was saying and your mind wandered or your eyes glazed over, you are not alone. The following list should help.

First, what is accounting really. **Accounting** is not just recording your revenues and expenses. It is a total system that tracks all your transactions, uses the data to create reports that show the financial health of your business and can be used in all areas of your businesses, for example: operations, marketing, human resources, to make and keep your business successful.

Bookkeeping is the process of entering data into an accounting system which can be manual or computerized. These items include the amount, date, and sources of each revenue and expense as well as determining if something is an asset, something you own like cash, or a liability which is something you owe, like sales tax.

Assets are highly desirable. They add value to your business. This can be cash, accounts receivables (someone owes you money), property such as a building, equipment such as computers and cars, or investments like stocks or bonds.

Liabilities are usually not desirable. They mean that you owe money to someone and that takes away value from your business. They can be a vendor for supplies, credit cards for operations, especially in the beginning or possibly a mortgage (that building again). And of course, your state or federal government for taxes payable. The only good thing about liabilities is that you can use OPM (other people's money) to leverage your start and the growth of your business, as long as the terms of the financing are not more than they are worth.

Equity or capital is the difference between assets and liabilities. Now you obviously want your assets to exceed your liabilities although in the start-up phase, this may not be the case. In other words, **you** are paying for things out of your own pocket to keep the business going

Revenues are again highly desirable. They represent all your sales less any returns, chargebacks or anything you need to produce items for sale. if you have physical inventory, you will also have what's called cost of goods and this is deducted from revenue to get your net revenue. Your cost of goods could be as simple as for example: you sell coffee mugs and the cost of the coffee mug and the printing on it is outsourced, or it could be as complicated as you do t-shirts and you don't outsource them so you embroider them or you paint on them or whatever so then you've got the cost of your art supplies as well as your actual physical product the t-shirt that goes into your cost of goods.

Expenses are not desirable, but you can't live without them. They represent all the things that cost you money to stay in business. There are two types of expenses: those related to your sales and those related to general operations. Those related to sales are what we called cost of goods. The others are the operational stuff are like postage, if you have an autoresponder service that's an expense, if you take credit cards and they charge you fees, which everybody does, those are all operational expenses. So, in other words you have to spend the lovely green stuff to make more green stuff.

Now every category can be broken down into dozens of subcategories, but again I don't want those eyes to glaze over. I hope this brief overview helps.

Now the one thing you can do with just these five terms is create three main sets of financials: your General Ledger, your Income Statement and your Balance Sheet. These are the things you will need for bankers and for the IRS. Now with these financials, there are numbers you can pull off of them and create ratios, Ratios are an easy way to see how well you are doing other than whether on your income statement it says positive or negative. Some standard ratios are your ROI or Return on Investment (net income/average investment), current ratio (current assets/current liabilities) or the quick ratio also known as the acid-test ratio (quick assets/current liabilities) which only uses cash or other liquid assets, not inventories or fixed assets such as buildings or equipment.

Conclusion

Well, it's been a short, but I hope interesting and informative ride through this Basic Guide to Accounting. Accounting is not hard, but it's not easy either, especially if numbers are not your thing.

You may choose to do your own books, or you may decide to hire someone to do your books. But whatever you decide to do you can now make an informed decision that is best for you and for your business.

Now, if you feel like you would like more information and/or training, I'm here to help.

Please visit **www.MyAccounting911.com** for more information on my series of training videos that covers all this information and more in greater detail. But no matter what decision you make, there is always help to be found.

Good Luck and Happy Accounting!

Exhibits

Exhibit A:

ABC Company
2018

date	desc	total	cash	chase cc	equity	interest income	product	c of g	rent	contract payroll	R & M	profit s
Jun-18	Beginning Balance	0.00	132,196.17	(759.42)	(192,630.08)	(0.04)	(319,707.27)	80,583.75	18,000.00	74.67	520.55	5,909.77
	sales- cash	-	20,213.86				(20,213.86)	2,324.59				
	sales- Combined	-	2,545.00				(2,545.00)	292.68				
	profl fee	-	(650.00)									650.00
	util	-	(297.86)									
	contract payroll	-	(1,422.00)							1,422.00		
	ins/sales fees	-	(1,063.37)									
	auto	-	(945.69)									
	cc pymt	-	(50.00)									
	cc chg	-		(73.99)								
	current month activity	(0.00)	(105,678.02)	569.74	-	-	(75,118.90)	13,220.08	6,000.00	1,422.00	351.58	749.00
Jun-18	Ending Balance	0.00	26,518.15	(189.68)	(192,630.08)	(0.04)	(394,826.17)	93,803.83	24,000.00	1,496.67	872.13	6,658.77

Exhibit B:

ABC Company
Income Statement
For the Five Months Period Ending May 31, 2018

	MTD	YTD
Revenue		
Professional Income	650.00	3,250.00
Interest Income	-	-
Total Revenue	650.00	3,250.00
Expenses		
Professional	581.25	3,048.72
Bank Fees	15.00	60.00
Credit Card Interest	-	20.15
Loan Interest	218.85	1,213.28
Auto	-	26.97
Meals	-	101.35
Total Expenses	815.10	5,075.47
Net Income/(Loss)	(165.10)	(1,825.47)

Exhibit C:

ABC Company
Balance Sheet
As of May 31, 2018

Assets		
Current Assets		
Cash 1	2,214.20	
A/R Other	1,423.76	
Total Current Asssets		3,637.96
Long Term Assets		
Property	90,000.00	
Total Long Term Assets		90,000.00
Total Assets		93,637.96
Liabilities		
Current Liabilities		
CC 2	10,000.00	
WF Visa	(0.00)	
Total Current Liabilities		10,000.00
Long Term Liabilities		
Loan	55,474.12	
Total Long Term Liabilities		55,474.12
Equity		
my contributions	53,025.43	
Net Income/(Loss) PY	(23,036.12)	
Net Income/(Loss) CY	(1,825.47)	
Total Equity		28,163.84
Total Liabilities & Equity		93,637.96

About the Author

Nina Register is a CPA and has over 35 years of industry experience. Her specialties are general accounting, real estate accounting and small business accounting. She is a widow with a son and lives in Texas.

Please visit http://www.MyAccounting911.com to find out how else I can help you.